of the World

Asia

Australia

Locations of Animals Found in This Book

A giant anteater—Central and South America
B morpho butterfly—South America
C Parson's chameleon—Africa
D Amazon river dolphin—South America
E harpy eagle—Central and South America
F dart poison frog—South America
G mountain gorilla—Africa
H Hawaiian honeycreeper—Hawaiian Islands
I green iguana—Central and South America
J jaguar—Central and South America
K leaf katydid—Central and South America
L black and white ruffed lemur—Madagascar
M blue and yellow macaw—South America
N night monkey—South America
O okapi—Africa
P red-bellied piranha—South America
Q resplendent quetzal—Central America
R Sumatran rhinoceros—Southeast Asia
S three-toed sloth—South America
T keel-billed toucan—Central America
U red uakari—South America
V eyelash viper—Central America
W black forest wallaby—Australia
X xenops—Central and South America
Y yapok—Central and South America
Z zorro—South America

Key

tropical rain forests

THE LIVING RAIN FOREST

An Animal Alphabet

PAUL KRATTER

i🜂i Charlesbridge

For my biggest supporter, Tia, and my two boys, Joel and Marshall

Thank you:
The Oakland Zoo; San Francisco Zoo; San Diego Zoo; Los Angeles Zoo;
California Academy of Sciences; Museum of Vertebrate Zoology,
University of California, Berkeley; and especially my brother, Andy Kratter,
collection manager in ornithology, Florida Museum of Natural History
—P. K.

Animal lengths include entire body unless otherwise noted. Birds are measured from
the end of the beak to the end of the tail. Butterflies are measured by wingspan.

Text and illustrations copyright © 2004 by Paul Kratter
All rights reserved, including the right of reproduction in whole or in part in any form.
Charlesbridge and colophon are registered trademarks of Charlesbridge Publishing, Inc.

Published by Charlesbridge
85 Main Street
Watertown, MA 02472
(617) 926-0329
www.charlesbridge.com

Library of Congress Cataloging-in-Publication Data
Kratter, Paul.
The Living Rain Forest : an animal alphabet /
written and illustrated by Paul Kratter.
p. cm.
Summary: Introduces twenty-six rain forest animals from A to Z,
providing the name, favorite foods, and unique characteristics of each.
ISBN 1-57091-603-9 (reinforced for library use)
1. Rain forest animals—Juvenile literature. 2. English language—Alphabet—Juvenile literature.
[1. Rain forest animals. 2. Alphabet.] I. Title: Vanishing rain forest. II. Title.
QL112.K73 2004
591.734—dc21   2003003761

Printed in the United States of America
(hc) 10 9 8 7 6 5 4 3 2

Illustrations done in acrylics and watercolors on Strathmore watercolor board
Display type and text type set in Opti Caslon Antique, Tekton, New Baskerville
Color separations by ArtScans Studio, Inc., Manhattan Beach, California
Printed and bound by Lake Book Manufacturing, Inc., Melrose Park, Illinois
Production supervision by Brian G. Walker

Introduction

Rain forests cover only six percent of the earth's land yet contain over half its animal and plant species. This unique habitat is found around the world near the equator. A combination of high temperatures and heavy rainfall—at least 60 inches per year—creates a lush and diverse environment unlike any other.

Unfortunately this precious habitat is threatened by deforestation, global warming, and overhunting of bushmeat—wildlife from the African "bush," or forest, that is used for meat. In the past 200 years we have lost more than half the world's rain forests.

This book features just a few of the millions of species of animals found only in tropical rain forests. Some of these animals, like the jaguar and the macaw, are familiar sights. Others, like the uakari and the zorro, are so rare that little is known about them. Each animal has special adaptations to help it live in its environment. But like the rain forests they inhabit, all these creatures face extinction.

The Living Rain Forest can help people learn about the rare, diverse, and beautiful animal life of the rain forest and teach them to value it. If we grow to appreciate our rain forests, we can preserve them before it's too late.

A anteater

The giant anteater is toothless. It uses its long snout to locate ant nests or termite mounds. The anteater uses its powerful claws to tear open a mound and then lick up its meal with a long, sticky tongue.

GIANT ANTEATER
Myrmecophaga tridactyla
Body 3–4 feet, Tail 2–4 feet

B butterfly

The morpho butterfly sips the
nectar of flowers through its
proboscis. The brown undersides
of its wings are good camouflage
in the rain forest. As it flies, the
butterfly seems to appear and then
disappear against the background,
making it hard to catch.

Camouflage: *A pattern or disguise to hide something. Coloring or covering that allows animals to blend in with or hide in their surroundings.*

Proboscis: *A tubular projection from the mouth of an insect used for sucking.*

MORPHO BUTTERFLY
Morpho menelaus

Wingspan 3.5–4.5 inches

C chameleon

The Parson's chameleon has a long, sticky tongue that it uses to catch insects to eat. It changes colors if scared or to match its surroundings.

PARSON'S CHAMELEON

Chamaeleo parsoni

Length 29–35 inches

Ddolphin

The Amazon river dolphin has very small eyes. It uses echolocation to locate its prey swimming in murky water. It also pokes its head in the muddy river bottom to find crabs, fish, and turtles to eat.

Echolocation: *A way to locate an object using sound waves.*

AMAZON RIVER DOLPHIN
Inia geoffrensis

Length 6.5–8.5 feet

E eagle

The harpy eagle is armed with powerful feet, huge talons, and a strong beak. It swoops through the treetops hunting a variety of animals including monkeys, opossums, sloths, and snakes.

Talons: *Claws of a bird.*

HARPY EAGLE
Harpia harpyja
Length 34–36 inches

F frog

The dart poison frog's bright colors warn other animals that its skin is toxic. This tiny amphibian eats ants, termites, and other insects.

Amphibian: *Cold-blooded animal that has a backbone. Amphibians live in water and breathe with gills when young, but develop lungs and live on land as adults.*
Toxic: *Poisonous.*

DART POISON FROG
Dendrobates azureus

Length 1.5 inches

gorilla

The mountain gorilla is the largest, and one of the rarest, primates. It eats a wide variety of plants including bamboo, wild celery, roots, fruit, soft bark, and fungi.

Fungi: *Mushroom-type organisms that feed on decaying or dead material.*

Primates: *Mammals including man, apes, monkeys, and lemurs. Primates have large brains, forward-facing eyes, and five digits on each hand and foot.*

MOUNTAIN GORILLA
Gorilla gorilla beringei

Length 4.5–6.5 feet

H honeycreeper

The Hawaiian honeycreeper is found only on the islands of Hawaii. Its curved bill and brushlike tongue help it to gather nectar from flowers.

Nectar: *The sugary liquid of a plant that attracts insects, birds, and bats to pollinate.*

HAWAIIAN HONEYCREEPER
Vestiaria coccinea

Length 6 inches

I iguana

The green iguana is mainly arboreal, but it's also a good swimmer. The female lays up to 70 eggs in a nest buried in the ground.

Arboreal: *Lives in or spends a good deal of time in trees.*

GREEN IGUANA
Iguana iguana

Length 4–6 feet

jaguar

The powerful jaguar likes to swim and is a good tree climber. It hunts at night for a wide range of prey including deer, reptiles, and aquatic animals.

Aquatic: *Living or growing in water.*

JAGUAR
Panthera onca
Body 3.5–6.5 feet, Tail 18–30 inches

 katydid

The leaf katydid lies motionless during the day to hide from predators. It becomes active at night, feeding on leaves, shoots, and flowers.

Predator: *An animal that hunts other animals for food.*

LEAF KATYDID
Mimetica incisa

Length 1–2.5 inches

L lemur

The black and white ruffed lemur is a noisy primate. It will grunt and even roar when alarmed. Fruit, nectar, seeds, and leaves make up its diet.

BLACK AND WHITE RUFFED LEMUR
Varecia variegata variegata

Body 22 inches, Tail 3.5–4 feet

M macaw

The blue and yellow macaw uses its large hooked beak for eating fruit and for climbing in the canopy. This social bird is usually found in pairs and can be seen in flocks of up to 30 birds.

Canopy: *Sheltered area under the treetops.*

BLUE AND YELLOW MACAW
Ara ararauna

Length 35 inches

N

night monkey

The night monkey is nocturnal and has huge eyes that help it to see in the dark. It makes a soft hooting noise like an owl. The night monkey feeds on fruit, flowers, leaves, and insects.

Nocturnal: *Active at night.*

NIGHT MONKEY
Aotus trivirgatus
Body 12–16 inches, Tail 11.5–17.5 inches

okapi

The okapi feeds on leaves by stripping them from branches with its long prehensile tongue. This close relative of the giraffe is shy and rarely seen.

Prehensile: *Adapted for grabbing, especially by wrapping around.*

OKAPI
Okapia johnstoni

Length 6.5–7.5 feet

P
piranha

The red-bellied piranha lives in fresh water and hunts in schools. It will attack any animal splashing in the water. A piranha darts in and bites off small pieces of flesh with its sharp teeth.

School: *A group of the same kind of fish.*

RED-BELLIED PIRANHA
Serrasalmus nigrifronc

Length 6–8 inches

Q quetzal

The resplendent quetzal feeds
mainly on fruit but will also eat
small lizards and insects. The male
attracts a female by swooping
down from the canopy and letting
his long tail covert feathers flow
through the air.

Resplendent: *Shining brightly.*
Covert feathers: *Feathers covering the quills
of a bird's wings and tail.*

RESPLENDENT QUETZAL
Pharomachrus mocinno

Body 14 inches, Tail 25 inches

R rhinoceros

The shy Sumatran rhinoceros keeps itself cool and free of biting insects by rolling in mud. It feeds at night on vegetation near water. It is the smallest and hairiest kind of rhinoceros.

SUMATRAN RHINOCEROS
Dicerorhinus sumatrensis

Length 8.5–10 feet

Ssloth

The three-toed sloth is slow-moving. It spends the day hanging upside down feeding on leaves. Greenish algae growing on its fur help to hide the sloth from predators.

Algae: *Small plants that grow in water.*

THREE-TOED SLOTH
Bradypus infuscatus

Length 18–20 inches

T toucan

The keel-billed toucan's bill is lightweight and used to grab fruit, insects, and even the eggs of other birds. Both parents care for their young in a nest made in a hollow tree.

KEEL-BILLED TOUCAN
Ramphastos sulfuratus

Length 20 inches

Uuakari

The red uakari is a short-tailed monkey. Its strong jaws help it eat fruit with hard outer shells that other monkeys can't eat. The uakari lives in a large group of 20 to 30 animals.

RED UAKARI
Cacajao calvus rubicundus

Body 15–22.5 inches, Tail 5.5–7.5 inches

V viper

The eyelash viper will lie motionless waiting for a small bird or mammal to pass. The viper strikes quickly, using poison from its fangs to stop its prey.

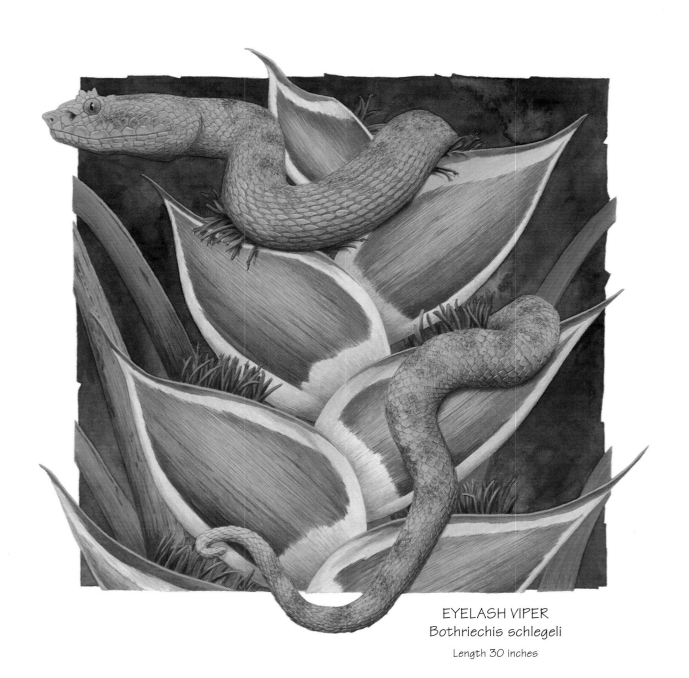

EYELASH VIPER
Bothriechis schlegeli

Length 30 inches

W

wallaby

The black forest wallaby is a marsupial. It gives birth to a small baby, called a joey, that develops fully in its mother's pouch. It feeds at night on many kinds of plants.

Marsupial: A mammal such as a kangaroo or opossum. The females have a pouch that serves to carry their young.

BLACK FOREST WALLABY
Dorcopsis atrata
Body 29–39 inches, Tail 11–15 inches

X xenops

The bill of the plain xenops is designed to peck and probe. The xenops climbs dead branches and vines looking for insects to eat.

PLAIN XENOPS
Xenops minutus

Length 5 inches

yapok

The yapok is a type of opossum. This aquatic marsupial has a pouch that can be closed tightly underwater. Webbed feet help the yapok swim as it hunts for fish, frogs, and other freshwater prey.

YAPOK
Chironectes minimus

Body 10–16 inches, Tail 12–17 inches

Z zorro

The zorro is a type of dog. It eats rodents, small mammals, and some plants. Very little is known about this rare creature.

Rodents: *Mammals with sharp teeth used for gnawing, such as mice, rats, squirrels, and beavers.*

ZORRO
Atelocynus microtis

Body 28–40 inches, Tail 9–13 inches

Emergent Layer—
Tallest trees can
reach 130 feet.

Canopy Layer—
These trees cut off
much of the sunlight
to the rest of the
forest. Trees measure
65 feet high or more.

Mid Layer—
Trees measure
15 to 65 feet.

Shrub Layer—
Vegetation here is
sparse compared to
canopy. Trees and
plants grow to 15 feet.

Ground Layer—
Fungi, ferns, herbs,
and small seedlings
are found here.

Resources

Organizations:

Rainforest Action Network
221 Pine Street, Suite 500
San Francisco, CA 94104
(415) 398-4404
www.ran.org

The Rainforest Alliance
665 Broadway, Suite 500
New York, NY 10012
(212) 677-1900
www.rainforest-alliance.org

Books:

Berger, Melvin, and Gilda Berger. *Does It Always Rain in the Rain Forest?: Questions and Answers About Tropical Rain Forests* (Scholastic Question and Answer Series). New York: Scholastic Reference, 2002.

Cherry, Lynne. *The Great Kapok Tree: A Tale of the Amazon Rain Forest.* San Diego, CA: Gulliver Books, 1990.

Cheshire, Gerard. *The Tropical Rainforest* (Nature Unfolds). New York: Crabtree Publishing Company, 2001.

Collard, Sneed B., III. *The Forest in the Clouds.* Watertown, MA: Charlesbridge, 2000.

Greenaway, Theresa. *Jungle* (Eyewitness Books). New York: DK Publishing, 2000.

Wilkes, Angela. *Rain Forest* (Question Time: Explore and Discover). Boston: Houghton Mifflin Co., 2002.

Willow, Diane. *At Home in the Rain Forest.* Watertown, MA: Charlesbridge, 1991.

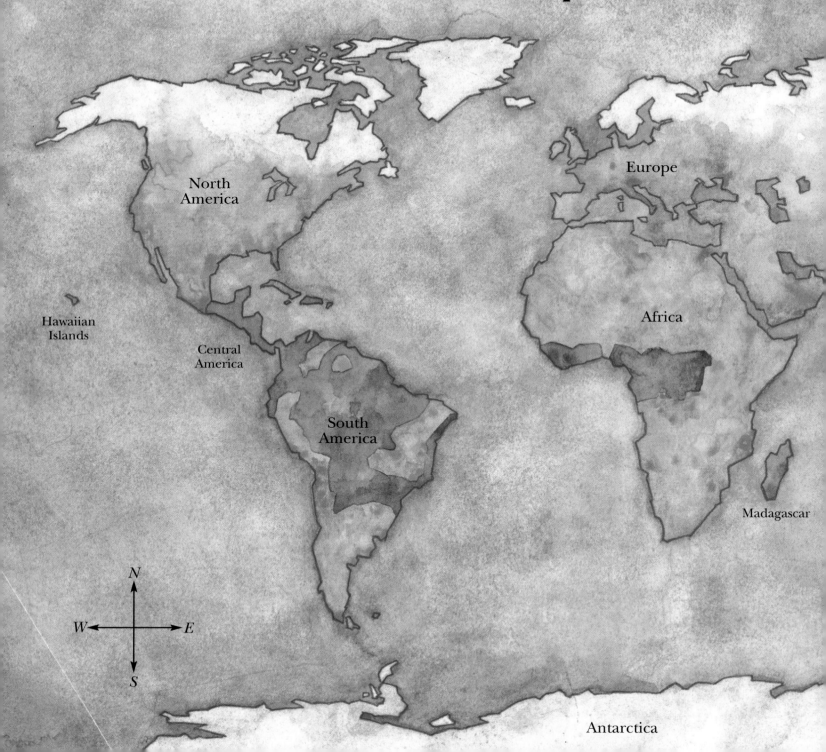

Tropical Rain Forests

North
America

Europe

Hawaiian
Islands

Central
America

Africa

South
America

Madagascar

N

W — E

S

Antarctica